# Finding a Way to Forgive

KELLI SANDERS

ISBN: 978-1-949106-94-7

Published by Word and Spirit Publishing
P.O. Box 701403
Tulsa, Oklahoma 74170
wordandspiritpublishing.com

# Endorsement

I have known Kelli Sanders for many years. She has worked by my side in the Philippines, and she continues her work with me in ministry to this day. She is a vital part of the MKMI ministry. I am very aware of the challenges she has faced in the realm of forgiveness, and I am deeply impressed with how she has taken the devil's best shot and rebounded stronger than ever for the Lord. Truly, she has walked the path this book presents. Unforgiveness is lethal poison from hell. We all need to know how to keep our hearts clean and free from this spiritual cancer. Kelli also knows I have been where this book goes. She was there when I faced some very tough choices in the area of forgiveness. By experience, I know this is a book of truth that many believers need to read and heed. If that includes you, I encourage you to begin the journey. There's no better time for that than now!

Apostle Mike Keyes Sr.

Founder & President

Mike Keyes Ministries International

# Contents

INTRODUCTION

# Taking the First Step

*And be kind to one another, tenderhearted, forgiving one another,* ***even as*** *God in Christ forgave you.*

—Ephesians 4:32 NKJV, emphasis mine

There are many books in the world on forgiveness, but I believe the assignment for this one is to help people who feel it may be impossible to forgive, those struggling to find a way to obey God's command to forgive. For many, forgiveness is not something that comes easily. It doesn't help that it isn't well understood. As Christ followers, the command to forgive is not something we take lightly, but it seems to be an elusive goal reserved for the "super spiritual," and for some, not even remotely possible. Maybe the book in your hands is just the tool the Holy Spirit needs to reach you where you are. That location might be on the other side of betrayal or loss. It might be in the middle of strife and pain. It might be looking at God's command and thinking, *There is no way He can expect forgiveness in* this *situation*.

In my personal journey through life's many "relationship roads," I have had great opportunities to navigate this path of forgiveness. Human relationships are messy. They don't come with Google maps, and we can't ask Alexa for all the answers to the problems they present to us, but we do have the Bible as our guide and the Holy Spirit as our Teacher. There are answers to be found. There is direction that will lead us straight out of the bondage that unforgiveness brings and right into the freedom that can be experienced when we walk in divine love.

Bringing you to that place of freedom is the reason I have written this book, and let's be honest, the level of strife, division, hate, judgment, and all the hardness these things can produce has increased exponentially in recent times. How do we move away from defaulting to judgment, criticism, and strife-filled conversations? How do we breach the divide and cultivate the God kind of love that brings healing, freedom, and, in the best-case-scenarios, unimaginable reconciliation?

This book is written with the hope that we will see a pathway forward. That we will learn what forgiveness is and what it is not. That the scales will fall from our spiritual eyes, and we will release the pain of offense, remove the root of bitterness, and truly find a way, not just to forgive in one situation, not just to forgive one person, but to cultivate a lifestyle of forgiveness. My prayer is that *love* becomes our default. That our words would be edifying, life-giving, and filled with grace. That we would apply the truth we discover in these pages, and that this would, in turn, effect change in our lives and in the lives of those around us.

The power of forgiveness is greater than we have imagined. If you can find a way to release that power in your life and live in the freedom that it brings, then this book will have accomplished God's purpose for it.

So, I invite you to start this journey with an open heart, believing that all things are possible with God.

# With God It Is Possible to Forgive

*Jesus replied, "What is impossible with man is* ***possible*** *with God."*

—Luke 18:27 NIV, emphasis mine

I remember sitting in an auditorium one evening watching a group of young boys and girls reenacting acts of violence that had been committed against them and their people. Young boys were stolen from their families, their parents were murdered, their sisters were taken as sex slaves. They were forced to become child soldiers and commit violent acts themselves. Through an amazing ministry—Watoto—they were introduced to Jesus and learned about the power of forgiveness. As they traveled the world to share their stories, process their trauma, and find healing, they helped people like me see the truth that forgiveness is the only way to truly be free. As each child came forward at the end, they would declare, "I forgive 'X' for murdering my mother." Or "I forgive 'X' for kidnapping my sister." I could hardly believe what I was hearing, and yet it was sincere, fueled by a sense that they had discovered the love of God and the Person of God. It begged the question, "Is it possible to forgive in every situation?"

We can all think of the extremes in which nobody would expect us to forgive "that" abuse or betrayal or offense. According to Scripture, we can do nothing in and of ourselves (John 15:5). This means that on our own, we can't find it within ourselves to forgive at all times. Forgiveness *can* seem impossible to extend in certain situations—but we are not on our own. As Jesus points out in Luke 18:27, what is impossible with man is very possible with God. Can we settle this point based on the words of Jesus? Allow me the liberty to go just a little further. If impossible things can become possible with God, let's ask the question of whether we are with God and whether God is with us. Isaiah 41:10 (NKJV) answers this beautifully:

> *"Fear not, for I am with you; be not dismayed, for I am your God. I will strengthen you, yes, I will help you, I will uphold you with My righteous right hand."*

The Word of God is alive and powerful (Hebrews 4:12). In this passage, God is communicating, making it real to us, that He is with us! Allow His words to enter your heart and pierce through the pain. There is truth here. There is healing and light and life in these God-breathed words. God is with you, and you are His, just as sure as He is yours. God will strengthen you. God will help you. God will hold you up when you feel like you can't stand on your own. This truth must be settled to the core of your being: "GOD IS WITH ME."

When our focus shifts from what we *can't* do on our own to what we *can* do with God, then we can begin to see the glimmer of hope that forgiveness *is* possible—even for the most grievous of offenses. Remember that we are walking on a path together throughout the pages of this book. I know you may have many internal objections right now. I know there may be intense emotion coursing through your veins when you allow your mind and heart to consider releasing a particular offender. You may find comfort and peace in knowing God is with you, but you are so hurt, so angry. I get that. I've been where you are. Maybe it's not the same in every way, but the fight to get to my freedom can shine a light on the path to yours.

I want you to do one thing with me right now as an act of faith. Pray and ask God to help you. If you feel it is impossible to forgive in your own strength, ask for help. He is a very present help in time of need. He *will* help you.

Say out of your mouth: "It is **possible** for me to forgive _________." (Insert the name of the person/people/group who hurt you.) Even if you say it through gritted teeth with anger in your heart, even if you say it with tears in your eyes and doubts in your mind—it is a baby step in God's direction. Let's keep walking it out.

CHAPTER 1

# A Willing Heart

*Therefore, my beloved, as you have always obeyed, not as in my presence only, but now much more in my absence, work out your own salvation with fear and trembling;* ***for it is God who works in you both to will and to do for His good pleasure.***

—Philippians 2:12–13 NKJV, emphasis mine

Sometimes we don't have the will to do what God commands us to do. We are just trying to get to a place where we are willing to be willing if God would help us to get there. Maybe that is right where you are today. The beautiful thing about living in God's amazing grace is that it fills in the gaps of our growth. Not everyone can lean on the experiences they have with God, or the revelation of what Christ did for them when called upon to forgive. We are all at different levels of spiritual growth, but God knows right where we are. His grace is more than enough to create bridges for us to walk on when our "growth gaps" leave us feeling unable to do what His Word requires. Even if we have great experiences in God and great revelation of His truth, it can still require great grace to overcome certain offenses. I recall Joyce Meyer saying often, "New level, new devil." So, even as we grow in Christ, the potential for offense seems to grow right along with us. Wherever each of us lands in our level of spiritual maturity, the wonderful truth is that God's grace is enough to keep us going and keep us growing.

Knowing this, I invite you to open your heart to Him and trust that He's got you as you walk out this forgiveness journey. I continually refer to it as a "journey" because it is not a onetime event. It is a decision to obey God's Word that, in turn, starts a process with God Himself. What a masterful heart surgeon He is! What a skilled and compassionate Counselor. He isn't mad at you because you can't, "Just get over it." Yes, sometimes we wallow in self-pity over trivial things, and we need someone to snap us out of our foolish two-year-old tantrums, BUT not all situations are the same. It is very disheartening to me when I hear people say, "Just get over it." If you're mad that someone sat in your seat at church, you probably need to hear those words, but when you are looking for real answers on how to obey God's command to forgive someone who stole your innocence as a child or betrayed you in marriage or violated you and physically abused you, or someone who harmed your children, then the admonition to "just forgive them" is not helping you. In addition, piling on guilt for not being able to "just get over it" doesn't help, either. What does truly help is knowing that God is longsuffering, patient, and kind. He isn't tapping His foot and looking at the clock, wondering when you are going to get your act together and just forgive already. No. He is so tender in heart, and He sees all of you. He knows the entire story, and He knows where you are in your knowledge of the Word. He is the perfect Teacher, and He won't give you a failing grade on a test if He knows you haven't been given the chance to learn the material yet. If you trust in His goodness, I believe it will help you take the first step of being willing to be willing to forgive.

In Philippians 2:12–13, Paul is concluding his appeals to the Philippians to be like-minded and humble, to look out for each other and work out their own salvation through obedience to God. He is telling them to actively pursue spiritual maturity, recognizing and reverencing God by continually looking at their own heart to make sure it remains pure in His sight. Paul refers to them as his "beloved," which tells us they are dear to him. He is saying all of this in love because, like a good father, he wants them to live in the fullness of God's goodness as his spiritual children. He then empowers them with this truth: It is not their own willpower on which they should rely to work out this amazing salvation. It is God Himself at work *in* them, creating in them *the will,* or *the desire,* to do what is pleasing to Him. Wow! What a gift!

Why am I telling you this? The goal of our Christian growth is not to survive, but to thrive in this world, and in our thriving, to lead others to that same abundant, thriving life. Just as Paul spoke to the Philippian church with the heart of a father and told them how to live a life that was pleasing to God, our Father God is speaking to us today, giving us that same instruction. What's more, He is telling us how to do it. We don't do it in our own willpower or strength. We do it by looking to God inside of us, whom we know is at work in us, creating the desire not only to be *willing* to do what He says, but to actually do it.

This is good news, my friends. When we read God's command to forgive, we can know that even if we don't currently have the desire or the will to do it, we can look to God and trust what He has said in His Word. He delights when we reach out with our faith and declare, "God, I may have zero desire in my heart to obey Your command to forgive this offender, but Your Word says that You are at work in me creating that desire and creating the willingness within me to do it. You are a good Father, and You only want my best, so I trust You and I believe what You have said. Create in me the will and desire to do what Your Word requires." When you reach out to God in this way, His Spirit gets to work and responds to your faith! *Forgiveness is an act of faith!* It is not confirmed by our feelings. It is a choice. In the next chapter, we are going to look at the power of the quality decision to forgive.

## CHAPTER 2

# Forgiveness Is a Choice

*"I call heaven and earth to witness against you that today I have set before you life or death, blessing or curse. Oh, that you would* **choose** *life; that you and your children might live!* **Choose** *to love the Lord your God and to obey him and to cling to him, for he is your life and the length of your days. You will then be able to live safely in the land the Lord promised your ancestors, Abraham, Isaac, and Jacob."*

—DEUTERONOMY 30:19–20 TLB, EMPHASIS MINE

There is something beautiful and liberating about having a free will. Having a free will means that you and I are given the responsibility of choice. We can decide as adults where we will live, what we will wear, with whom we will be friends, when we will retire, and the list goes on and on. It is simultaneously sobering at times to know the great responsibility that comes with our freedom to choose. It adds more weight to our decisions because we can't point fingers at someone else when our choices lead to negative consequences.

I remember believing as a teenager that I would raise my children without limits. They would be free to choose for themselves! I wouldn't put any boundaries on their lives! Of course, freedom-starved teens think that the "good life" comes once they have no boundaries and have the right to make all the decisions. What is not often considered in the teen years is the responsibility that comes with that freedom. Quite often, the freedom is wanted, but the responsibility is not.

*The most significant decision any human being will ever make is the choice to receive or to reject the salvation offered through Jesus Christ.* What a weighty decision to entrust to a human being! This alone is a great revelation of the value that God places on our freedom and free will. What a magnificent truth—that the God who created us and redeemed us then turns around and bestows absolute freedom on us and says, "You are free. Now it is your choice whether you will trust Me to be your Lord." What kind of radical love would lay down its life for those who may never even choose to love in return?

In Deuteronomy 30:19–20, we can hear the heart of God to His people as He implores them to choose life and blessing, safety and length of days, by simply loving and obeying Him. What did this choice require above all else? It required them to trust Him. Anytime we make a quality decision to obey God and do what His Word teaches us, it requires trust. It requires faith. *Does God really have my best interest in mind? Do His ways really lead to freedom, or are they unjust requirements that are impossible to keep, delivered to me by a distant and uncaring task master?*

This is a good moment to pause and reflect on what your perception of God is. How you perceive His character, nature, and trustworthiness will absolutely affect whether you are willing to surrender your life to Him and obey His Word. Is His command to forgive unjust, or is there something waiting for you on the other side of this decision that will bring blessing, life, safety, and length of days?

We talked in the previous chapter about God working in us to create the will and desire to do what His Word requires. The significance of having a willing heart is that it creates a hearing ear. Have you ever had the experience of talking to someone who really isn't listening? They are listening, but they don't hear. Jesus taught us to be aware of how we hear.

> *Then He said to them, "Pay attention to what you hear. By your own standard of measurement [that is, to the extent that you study spiritual truth and apply godly wisdom] it will be measured to you [and you will be given even greater ability to respond]—and more will be given to you besides."*
>
> —MARK 4:24 AMP

There is a connection between right hearing and right choosing. When our heart is in a posture of willingness to obey, and our ears are attuned to the truth that the Holy Spirit is attempting to get across to us, we can then receive that truth as an empowerment to choose obedience rather than defiance. We are empowered to exercise our freedom of choice with wisdom, being fully aware that with the freedom to choose comes the responsibility of owning our decisions. We need to be able to hear from God on this path of forgiveness. It is vitally important that we don't just listen to God, but really hear Him and apply His truth. It is only in this context that we will continue to be given the greater ability to respond to and receive from the riches of His goodness toward us.

I've had ample opportunity in my life to practice what I just described. One moment sticks out to me as offering a life-altering decision to forgive that would in turn affect the next days, months, and years of my life. I won't go into great detail about this life experience, but there was abuse, betrayal, devastating loss, and the grief that followed. I want to jump here to the time immediately after these events, when I came face-to-face with whether I would choose the path of forgiveness or bitterness.

I was attending a conference in which the theme was God's "amazing grace." At the time I was so freshly hurt and violated that I didn't even like to think of God's grace or mercy, because that would mean the offender in this situation could possibly be in a position one day to receive it! I was grieving and angry and processing great trauma with God. As I sat in the seat of this auditorium, there came a point in the service when the minister directed the ushers to begin passing the communion elements. I was about to take communion in remembrance of the blood Jesus shed to forgive me of my sins and His body, which was broken for my healing. I was at a crossroads. I remember sitting in that chair weeping because I felt the tender presence of God prompting me to move in the direction of forgiveness. I knew I could choose to justify my anger. I knew I could choose to ignore His voice. I knew I could choose to walk out because it was too hard. I also knew that if I did any of those things it would hinder my healing and harden my heart. I knew I would become dull of hearing, and my conscience would begin the searing process. I knew I would lay the sweetness of God's presence on the altar, sacrificing

His healing power so I could cling to my right to be offended. Here was the place where my freedom to choose bumped right up against my responsibility to own the decision I would now make. What was I going to do?

I cried for so long in that chair that a woman beside me put her hand on my shoulder and comforted me, not knowing the reason for my tears but wanting to be the love of God to me in that moment. I finally stood to my feet. I had a heart that was *willing* to be willing. I made the decision to forgive and took communion over it by faith. My feelings didn't change. My anger didn't subside. It wasn't the end of the journey by any means. It was the beginning of a beautiful walk that I was willing to take with my Savior. The immediate blessing was knowing I had the presence and power of the heart Healer with me. I didn't have all the answers, but I had the wisest Counselor within me, assuring me that this simple act of faith was enough to get started.

We aren't the only ones who weep. There were times when Jesus wept, too. Do you know what He wept over in Matthew 23? Do you know what would bring the Master to such a place of grief in His soul? Here we find it written out in detail:

> *O Jerusalem, Jerusalem—you are the city that murders your prophets! You are the city that stones the very messengers who were sent to deliver you! So many times I have longed to gather a wayward people, as a hen gathers her chicks under her wings—but you were too stubborn to let me.*
>
> —MATTHEW 23:37 TPT

Jesus was sent to a wayward people. They needed Him. His desire was to love them and protect them the way a mother protects her children. He longed to gather them to Himself, but they were too stubborn to let Him. His way would have led them to true life and peace, but they would not follow His way. Where this translation uses the word "longed," the verb used in the Greek is the word *thelo*. It carries the meaning of "being willing or desiring." In other words, He was willing, but they were *not willing,* and in His eyes, this was a tragedy. The Savior stood in their midst, and they didn't recognize Him. Their unwilling, stubborn hearts created dull ears that couldn't hear the truth, which led to them wrongly choosing death over life, curses rather than blessing. No wonder He wept. All they had to do was be willing to *let Him* help.

What about you? Are you in a place where you can begin to see the power of a willing heart that would hear God's truth and decide to forgive as an act of faith? Let Him help you. Allow Him the access to your heart so He can begin to mend and heal. This journey is about more than just forgiveness. It's about the relationship with Jesus that grows through trust and faith in the midst of unthinkable pain and loss. It's about Him having walked in our shoes, knowing our humanity. This way, when He returned to divinity, He could have true compassion and empathy born from His own experiences of temptation, betrayal, loss, grief, and death. He identifies with our suffering! We also identify with His suffering. This is one way in which we know each other deeply and personally. Let's talk more about this relationship in the next chapter.

## CHAPTER 3

# Forgiveness Is About Relationship

> ***That I may know Him** and the power of His resurrection, and the fellowship of His sufferings, being conformed to His death, if, by any means, I may attain to the resurrection from the dead.*
>
> —PHILIPPIANS 3:10–11 NKJV, EMPHASIS MINE

With God, it is all about relationship. His forgiveness of our sin and His laying it on Jesus was the only way to reconcile the world back to Himself, and He was willing to do whatever it took to make that happen. John 3:16 informs us that it was His love that was the motive for His giving of Jesus. Anyone who has children knows that love for them creates action. Love does. Love reaches. Love seeks. Love protects.

The God kind of love is personal, intimate, and real. God's love sees you and seeks to know you. As God's beloved children, we live and move and have our being in Him. This relationship trumps everything else. It is the highest priority.

God wants to meet us in our places of deepest brokenness, but He doesn't want pain and brokenness to become our identity. Sadly, some people want to hold on to their pain more than they want to step into their freedom. We cannot put our relationship with God on the altar in order to hold on to our pain. We must put our pain on the altar in order to hold on to our relationship with God. When delayed obedience begins to tear at the fabric of our relationship with God, we must get our priorities back in order. Relationship with God is first. When we sense the hardness that unforgiveness begins to cultivate in our heart, we must get our priorities back in order. Fellowship with God must be protected. When a root of bitterness begins to sour all our interactions, we must get our priorities back in order. We must run to the Father!

Making our relationship with God our greatest pursuit doesn't just help us let go of pain and trauma; it doesn't just empower us to choose forgiveness, but it is how we grow deeper in intimacy and union with Him. In Philippians 3, Paul is communicating how his pursuit of Christ revealed to him that everything in his life prior to knowing Christ was worth nothing. In comparison to knowing Him, nothing else mattered. None of his earthly accomplishments. None of his heritage or tradition. None of the "loss" he experienced could compare to what he gained in knowing Christ. He wanted to know Him above all else. He wanted to know not only the power of His resurrection but also the fellowship of His sufferings. How can we fully know Christ if we don't also share in the suffering He experienced? To be clear, I am not talking about suffering in sickness or poverty; I am talking about the suffering of obedience—the suffering of, "Not my will, God, but Yours be done." Simple obedience is hard. There is a suffering involved when it goes against our own will, but in that suffering, we get to know Christ in a deeper way.

When we obey the command to forgive and choose to walk in God's love, we identify with the One who prayed for those who were persecuting Him, the One who pled for mercy to come to those nailing Him to the cross, the One who served and loved day after day even when He was rejected and scorned. When we understand that forgiveness is not just about doing what God said, but it is about living in a trust relationship with another Person, it's about knowing Christ in a deeper way, then we won't sacrifice that precious fellowship and deep knowledge of God to follow our own will. We won't identify with our pain; we'll identify with God. We won't seek our own justice; we will seek the God who is just and trust His judgments. We won't choose hardness and bitterness over God's tenderness and mercy. When we know this wonderful, beautiful, holy God, all the things that try to bind us will lose their power. The anger, the hurt, the lies—they will all fall in His Presence. It is in this Presence that we truly begin to discover freedom and embrace a life of surrender.

CHAPTER 4

# Forgiveness Is About Freedom

*Stand fast therefore in the liberty by which Christ has made us free, and* ***do not be entangled again*** *with a yoke of bondage.*

—GALATIANS 5:1 NKJV, EMPHASIS MINE

God places a very high value on freedom. As mentioned earlier, He purchased our freedom with His own blood and then gifted us with the free-will choice to love and serve Him or deny and reject Him. He will not control anyone. He will not force His creation to come under His Lordship. The enemy of our soul, the devil, is the controller, the coercer, the one who enslaves through sin. The devil entraps through deception, manipulation, and lies. It is Christ who brings freedom through light and truth. In Galatians 5:1

we are exhorted to stand fast in the liberty for which Christ has made us free. The primary reference here is to avoid the bondage that results from trying to be justified by the law rather than being justified through faith in Christ, but God does not want us entangled with *any* yoke of bondage. The picture here of a "yoke" is one of an object that couples two things together. When two oxen are joined together, the yoke is around the neck of both animals. Imagine then the spiritual application of being tied to—or coupled together—with a law you could never fulfill, or the sin designed to destroy you. None of us would willingly tie ourselves to something that destroys us and enslaves us, *yet unforgiveness does just that.*

There is a saying, "Unforgiveness is like drinking poison yourself and waiting for the other person to die." Unforgiveness and bitterness in all forms will destroy us from the inside out.

There is a striking example in nature of the power of forgiveness. We find it in the oyster. When an irritant or parasite enters the oyster shell, it secretes a substance called *nacre*, also known as mother-of-pearl. This substance is a *response* to the intrusion. It encases the irritant in order to protect the *oyster*. This is how pearls are formed. If the oyster failed to produce nacre, the irritant that found its way inside would begin to cut into the tender flesh of the oyster and destroy the oyster from the inside until only a dried-out shell remained.

Forgiveness is the spiritual equivalent of nacre. When offenses enter our tender heart, we can respond with forgiveness–which ultimately protects us by encasing the bitterness that unforgiveness produces—but if we don't respond to the wounds of life with forgiveness, the bitterness eats away at us from the inside until our once-tender heart becomes hardened and hallow. The beautiful thing is that a pearl is essentially a healed wound. We can produce pearls from our wounds, or we can allow our wounds to destroy us. It is a powerful picture to me and a beautiful truth that an oyster that is never wounded can never produce pearls. We serve a God who gives beauty for ashes—a God who makes pearls from our wounds! He can redeem any pain we have experienced and turn it around, if only we will trust Him!

My dear friend, forgiveness is not about obeying a command from a God who doesn't understand what you've been through. It's about you living in freedom, healed and whole. Forgiveness and freedom are inseparable. Likewise, unforgiveness and bondage are inseparable. I don't believe any of us wants to live in bondage. The truth is, many times we just don't know how to get free. We don't realize how a baby step toward God results in a tremendous outpouring of grace. It is the power of a seed. All He needs is a tiny seed of faith and obedience to grow great grace in your life.

I pray that you are beginning to see, without question, why the path of forgiveness is the only choice for the child of God. He wants you to live in the freedom that Christ died for you to have. You and I want to live in that freedom! The only thing that would keep us out of that freedom is our own choice to be yoked together with a soul-destroying heart condition called unforgiveness. The only thing that would lead us to such a foolish choice is ignorance about forgiveness. Let's not be ignorant. Let's find out what forgiveness means. More importantly, let's find out what it does *not* mean. We will examine this in Part Two of this book.

# Wrong Beliefs About Forgiveness

*And you shall know the truth, and the truth* ***shall make you free.***

—JOHN 8:32 NKJV, EMPHASIS MINE

I can look back now and see just how many wrong beliefs I had about forgiveness as I navigated relationships in my young adult life. All this misinformation led to subjecting myself to pain, abuse, and betrayal. Then, because of the hurt, I fought the only true path to freedom that God provided. The devil is a master deceiver!

So many people believe wrongly about forgiveness, and it is costing them. They lose peace. They lose freedom. They lose health in their bodies. They lose the ability to trust, but it doesn't have to be this way. In John 8:32, Jesus reveals what makes us truly free. It is the truth. God's Word is truth, and when we live in His truth, we experience His freedom. We experience His love. We experience His joy and peace.

Let's look at several myths concerning forgiveness. I believe that as we dissect these false narratives around forgiveness, scales will fall from your eyes. I believe that what started as an act of faith, what began as "baby steps" as we launched this journey, will now grow into brave, confident movement toward your freedom—toward your good God.

CHAPTER 5

# Myth #1: Forgiveness Is Equal to Trust

Bob is married to Lisa and has a track record of unfaithful actions. Lisa discovers one evening that Bob has betrayed her trust again. Lisa, being a woman who loves God, knows the Bible instructs her to forgive. Over the next few weeks, she comes to a decision in her heart to forgive the broken trust. Unaware that trust and forgiveness are not the same, she grants Bob full trust again when she decides to forgive him. Because full trust is extended without accountability or boundaries, Bob continues to hurt Lisa with a pattern of betrayal. As the cycle of forgiveness, trust, broken trust, and pain continues, she doesn't understand how a loving God could expect her to subject herself to this pain over and over. Forgiveness feels to her like a heavy burden, a weakness that makes her easy prey for abuse.

Let's tear down this lie. Forgiveness and trust are not the same. When we make the choice to forgive it *does not require* that we place trust back in the offender. Forgiveness and reconciliation are not the same. When we make the choice to forgive, it *does not require* that we maintain a relationship with the one whom we have forgiven. Reconciliation may be possible, but in many cases, it isn't—and that's okay. Anytime the will of another person is involved, there is much that is not within our control.

Let's look to Jesus as our example. Jesus walked in perfect love and was the express image of God in the earth (Hebrews 1:3). His life of forgiveness is the example for us to follow as believers, and yet we read in the Word that He did not place His trust in those who were not trustworthy.

> *Because of the miraculous signs Jesus did in Jerusalem at the Passover celebration, many began to trust in him. But Jesus didn't trust them because he knew all about people. No one needed to tell him about human nature, for he knew what was in each person's heart.*
>
> —John 2:23–25 NLT

If any human will be trusted, that trust must be earned. Ultimately, we should only entrust our whole heart and being to one—that is, God. Apart from God, our trust is extended to those who must earn our trust through a history of trustworthy actions. When trust is broken through betrayal, trust should not be extended again until actions have changed, and hearts have changed. Forgiveness, however, can be extended at any point in time, because forgiveness is a choice to release the offender to God.

Let's return to Bob and Lisa's story. If Lisa knew the truth, it would empower her to forgive God's way. It would empower her to release her husband to God so God could deal with his heart. It would empower her to establish a clear expectation that Bob must earn her trust before she makes herself vulnerable to him again. Lisa would see God in a clearer light, obeying His command to forgive, and thanking Him for valuing her heart and protecting it from abuse. The truth would enable her to forgive, and with that forgiveness would come greater freedom.

I've known of far too many situations where the "forgiveness card" is used by abusers within the context of Christian relationships. This card is used to gain trust again, rather than a repentant heart that has truly changed. Maybe you have known of situations like these or have been in the context of these types of relationships yourself. By the grace of God, the truth about forgiveness is empowering you!

Well, what about Jesus' instruction to Peter to forgive the sins against him up to "seventy times seven" times? When this instruction to Peter is distilled down to the heart of the matter, Jesus was saying that we are to always live in forgiveness. There is never a time when it is okay not to forgive. Forgiveness is huge to God—it is the core of the Christian life. If someone we know gossips about us every chance they get—like seventy times seven times—we forgive them. What we *don't do* is become vulnerable to them and tell them our deepest heart issues, then act surprised when we find that our secrets are circulating among the masses. We live in forgiveness toward all, but we only extend trust to those who have proven themselves to be trustworthy.

CHAPTER 6

# Myth #2: Forgiveness Means What They Did Was Okay

Forgiveness is not cheap. It did cost something. Forgiveness never excuses the sin that made it necessary in the first place. Just as the forgiveness offered through Christ does not make sin okay, the forgiveness we extend to others does not make the sin they committed against us okay. Somehow we have come to believe, *If I forgive this person, it's like I'm saying what they did was okay.* Let's eliminate this false belief so it doesn't hinder your healing and keep you from moving forward.

When we forgive, what we are truly saying is, "What you did was not okay—it hurt, it cost me something, it affected me—but the *judgment* for what you did belongs to God, so I am releasing the debt." The true meaning of the word "forgiveness" (*aphiemi*) used in the Lord's Prayer is "to send away," or "to let go or leave something" (Matthew 6:9–13). This is what Jesus tells us to do with the sins committed against us. In this prayer, we ask God to let go of our sins or trespasses, and we let go of the sins or trespasses committed against us. We release them. We send them away. They are not ours to judge.

Isn't it tempting to hold on to the offenses committed against us? To nurse the wound and hold the grudge? When there is real hurt, it's hard to "let go" and trust that God will judge the situation correctly. There is something deep within us—a cry for justice—that desires the wrong to be made right through punishment. There is a place for both justice and mercy in the heart of God. We must believe that He knows the appropriate hour to execute justice and the right time to extend mercy. He knows the heart of every human and sees things we don't see.

> *Nothing in all creation is hidden from God. Everything is naked and exposed before*

> *his eyes, and he is the one to whom we are accountable.*
>
> —Hebrews 4:13 NLT

Each of us is accountable to the God who sees and knows everything—including all the secret and hidden things of the heart. We can trust Him to do what is right in every situation. That's why letting go of our right to be judge, jury, and executioner is actually a weight lifted off of our shoulders. When we send the offense away, we also send away the heavy burden it placed on our shoulders. We aren't saying the sin is okay, but we gladly give God the rightful place to carry the burden of judging it. His shoulders are bigger than ours!

## CHAPTER 7

# Myth #3: Forgiveness Means They Will "Get Away with It"

*Don't be misled—you cannot mock the justice of God. You will always harvest what you plant. Those who live only to satisfy their own sinful nature will harvest decay and death from that sinful nature. But those who live to please the Spirit will harvest everlasting life from the Spirit.*

—Galatians 6:7–8 NLT

There are always consequences for our actions. Period. Even when God's mercy is poured out over a situation, there can still be a "harvest of decay and death" from the things sown "in the flesh." When King David committed adultery and murder, God forgave him. David recognized his sin was against God (Psalm 51:4). He repented in sackcloth and ashes. He didn't eat. With his face to the ground, he begged God for mercy.

God was merciful to David. In fact, He later called him a man after His own heart. He was even mightily used of God. That doesn't mean there weren't very serious consequences for David's actions. Sin always brings forth death of some kind (James 1:15). Sometimes the price for sin is terribly high. The sword did not depart from David's house. His sons rebelled against him. His wives were given to other men. The child born to him and Bathsheba died. His sin had a ripple effect that touched all those who were connected to him.

This should serve as a reminder to all of us that there is the wonderful, washing, cleansing blood of Jesus to wipe away our sin, but that the amazing pardon we receive should never be taken lightly. It should never be an excuse to live a sinful life! Sin "pays back" with death, destruction, loss of purpose, loss of freedom, shame, guilt, and painful consequences. Nobody ever truly "gets away with it."

Recall again the words found in Hebrews 4:13, that we all give an account to the God who sees all. Whether in this life or the next, we all answer to God. Aren't you thankful for His mercy? Thank God that for those of us who receive the salvation offered through Jesus, there is an account given of our works so God can reward us. Those who die having rejected the salvation offered through Jesus, however, will give an account for their sin—they will "pay for it" because they chose not to receive the payment Jesus made on their behalf (Hebrews 10:30).

When we recognize how serious the consequences of sin can be—whether in this life or the next—it can even birth mercy in our own heart toward an offender. With the love of God shed abroad in our heart, and the awareness of both the goodness and the severity of God (Romans 11:22), we can pray for our enemies. We can forgive, knowing it doesn't mean people will "get away with" sin. It means *we* aren't making them pay for it. The sin will have a "payback" of its own. We are even positioned to get to a place in our own heart where we recognize in holy fear and awe just how much we have been forgiven of, and how great God's mercy was toward us. From this heart posture, we can sow mercy toward those headed for the painful consequences their sin has produced.

*I pray that we could all get to this place of humility—Holy Spirit, open our eyes! I pray that we would know by the Spirit the depth of God's grace toward us! That we would recognize how much we have been spared. God loves us so much. The debt of our sin was so great. Help us, Lord, to comprehend the reality that we could never pay our debt on our own. Never! Yet You forgave us. Help us to sow this same kind of love and mercy toward those who are headed for death and destruction. Help us to forgive, knowing how much we have been forgiven. In Jesus' name—Amen.*

CHAPTER 8

# Myth #4: Forgiveness Is Based on Feelings

Forgiveness is not a feeling. Forgiveness is a choice. We walk by faith and not by sight (2 Corinthians 5:7). Walking by sight means that we are looking to our five senses to confirm to us the reality of something. If we can see it, taste it, touch it, etc., then we know it is real. By contrast, walking by faith means that we are not relying on sensory experience to confirm the reality of something. We may not see it, smell it, or feel it, but that doesn't mean it isn't true or real. When it comes to forgiveness, too many are walking by sight. Too many wrongly believe that their feelings must instantly change if they have really forgiven someone. They believe the presence of anger and pain must mean that they haven't obeyed God's command to forgive.

Let's revisit my experience at the "Amazing Grace" conference I referred to in Chapter 2. It was there that I made a choice to forgive. It has been over a decade since that time, and I can still point back to it as a pivotal moment in my journey back to wholeness. Despite my choice to forgive, my feelings were not in line with what my heart decided to do. I had to "walk out" what I had declared by faith. I had been abused, betrayed, and discarded. That produced a lot of feelings in my soul that I had to take to God as each one came to the surface. The important truth is that feelings are taken to God so they can be processed *with* Him and filtered *through* Him.

God is a master Refiner. He is so loving and patient and kind. I have to say it again—He works with surgical precision on the heart. He knows *when* to help us cut away the bitter root. He knows *how* to extract it from the soul. He knows *where* to pour His healing balm, soothing tender areas until they become strong again. Natural wounds need time to heal. Heart wounds are no different. God knows it takes time for our feelings to catch up with what our heart has chosen to do by faith!

We don't judge whether forgiveness has taken place based on how we feel, and we don't wait until we "feel like" forgiving to make the decision to do so. Don't allow this misconception about forgiveness to hold you hostage to the lie that you aren't able to forgive. You are more than able to make a decision that leads you into a process that you "walk out" with God. You can do it.

## CHAPTER 9

# Myth #5: Forgiveness Means I Act Like It Never Happened

The Bible states that God will not remember our sins and our lawless deeds.

> *For I will be merciful to their unrighteousness, and their sins and their lawless deeds I will remember no more.*
>
> —Hebrews 8:12 NKJV

According to 1 Corinthians 13:5, we are told that love keeps no record of being wronged. God chooses not to remember, and we are instructed as people who walk in love not to keep records of suffered wrongs, so it is easy to see why some would assume that forgiveness means that we act like the sin or offense never happened.

We do have an instruction from the Word to investigate here, so let's look at the meaning of this verse. Does "keeping no record of being wronged" mean that we act like something never happened? This passage is also translated as, "does not take into account a suffered wrong." As an accounting term, it would mean that the suffered wrong is not put down on a person's account. The sin or offense is not imputed to them; they are not "charged" for it.

In the context of relationships, this means that we are not keeping score, tallying up offenses, ready to hold up, read, and rehearse our list when it is useful to our cause. Love doesn't keep a ledger full of debts owed to it. It is a way of life to keep the ledger at a zero balance.

When it comes to forgiving, it doesn't mean we forget. In fact, it is to our advantage to remember breaches of trust and abuses committed against us when it serves to keep us out of harm's way. In Matthew 10:6, Jesus instructs His disciples when He sends them out as sheep among wolves, to be wise as serpents and harmless as doves. Are there "wolves" in the world among the sheep? Absolutely there are. It requires wisdom to remain in the safety of the Shepherd's care as we coexist with wolves. It also requires an innocence and purity of heart to remain tender, and not allow the existence of the wolves in our midst to harden or corrupt us. The word for "harmless" used here literally means "umixed" or "pure"—there is no mixture of evil or guile. *There is an innocence about our heart, but* not *an ignorance.* We are instructed in the Word not to be ignorant of the devices and schemes used by the enemy or by whomever he works through to get to us.

Forgiveness does not mean we forget. It does not mean we act like it never happened. *It means we let go and we love.* We release debts, and we learn from what happened. We remain pure, but not ignorant. This is biblical forgiveness.

CHAPTER 10

# Myth #6: Forgiveness Requires an Apology

Have you ever been to jail? Have you ever been in a situation in which you felt trapped or bound? If you were imprisoned, whether physically or mentally, and I handed you the keys to your freedom, would you turn around and give them to the very person who put you in that mental or physical prison in the first place? Nobody in their right mind would do that unless they wanted to remain bound!

This is what it is like when we demand an apology before we are willing to forgive. We take the keys to our own freedom, and health, and life, and we hand them over to the person who, through their choice to abuse, betray, or hurt us, put us into the bondage of unforgiveness in the first place. Why would we give that power to them? Many people—not all, but many people—who have hurt us will go on with their lives indifferent, unrepentant, uncaring, and unwilling to acknowledge any wrongdoing. They aren't going to apologize or even feel bad for what they did. If you give that person the keys to your freedom, then you are giving them control over your destiny.

When we choose to forgive, in essence we are taking back the keys to our freedom. In truth, we are taking them back from Satan, because we do not wrestle against flesh-and-blood people (Ephesians 6:12), but against spiritual forces and influences *that operate through people.* We take our future out of the hands of our enemy and put it back into the hands of our good Father.

No, forgiveness does not require an apology, but it does require simple obedience. It requires trust in God's way of operating. His way is often contrary to our way. It's when we let go that we receive. It's when we lose our life that we find it. The way up is down. When we learn that God's ways are higher than ours, and His ways lead us to where we need to be, we can trust. We can release control, and it brings our life back under control. Let's place our whole heart and trust in the God who created us and who knows the good plans He has for our future (Jeremiah 29:11). He, more than any human being, is worthy of our trust.

# Living a Life of Forgiveness

*Jesus answered him, "The first of all the commandments is: 'Hear, O Israel, the* Lord *our God, the* Lord *is one. And you shall love the* Lord *your God with all your heart, with all your soul, with all your mind, and with all your strength.' This is the first commandment. And the second, like it, is this: 'You shall love your neighbor as yourself.'* **There is no other commandment greater than these**.*"*

—Mark 12:29–31 NKJV, emphasis mine

When we know the truth, we can walk in the truth. When we expose the lies that we believe about forgiveness, they lose their power over us. When we see clearly what biblical forgiveness is and why unforgiveness is so damaging to hold on to, we will gladly let it go and allow God the time and space to work in our situation. I pray there was a moment for you in Part Two of this book that opened your eyes and opened your heart to the true power of forgiveness.

In the last section of this book, we'll look at how to live a life of forgiveness, walking in the power of divine love on a daily basis. People can get very caught up in lists of commandments, but Jesus declared from the heart of the Father that love for God and love for others—*love*—is the greatest commandment of all. If we are going to be people of God who obey the law of love, we must find a way to forgive God, forgive ourselves, and forgive others. Before you break out your Bible to argue the idea that God needs forgiveness, let me share the heart of what is being said. Follow me into the last pages of this book.

CHAPTER 11

# Forgiving God

*"And you shall love the Lord your God with* ***all*** *your heart, with* ***all*** *your soul, with* ***all*** *your mind, and with* ***all*** *your strength."*

—MARK 12:30A NKJV, EMPHASIS MINE

I have stated over and over throughout this book that extending mercy and forgiveness requires trust in God. Jesus goes further and teaches us that the greatest commandment of all is to love God with our whole being—all our heart, soul, mind, and strength. So how do we do this when we believe that somewhere along the way God failed us? What if we feel that He wasn't there for us in a time of need, or He didn't do what we thought He should have done in different life situations? While I am not agreeing with the belief that He can fail us or needs our forgiveness, I am acknowledging that some people can allow the pain of disappointment, the grief over loss, or the inability to understand "why" something happened to erect a wall between their hearts and God. *If we blame Him for our pain, how can we go to Him for our healing?*

What does the Word say about God's heart toward us? It tells us that Jesus said this:

> *"The thief comes only in order to steal and kill and destroy. I came that they may have and enjoy life, and have it in abundance [to the full, till it overflows]."*
>
> —John 10:10 AMP

Has something been stolen from you? Has there been loss, or death, or destruction? There is a "thief" in this world. Satan is described as the thief, the deceiver, the accuser, the destroyer. God isn't the one bringing death or destruction. God is for you. He is not working against you. God loves you and will never leave you. **The Son of God** came that you might enjoy life in the fullness of the Spirit.

There are reasons things happen. Sometimes we make choices that lead us away from the Father and into sin, and sin can have consequences.

Sometimes, through no fault of our own, our lives collide with other people who choose to violate us through their choice to rebel against God and engage in evil. We currently live in a world where God's will is not always being done. That's why Jesus said to pray for God's Kingdom to come and for God's will to be done on earth as it is in heaven (Luke 11:2). How much crime is in heaven? None. How much pain and loss and violation of people is happening in heaven? Zero. Sometimes the people of God don't pray the way Jesus taught them to. My point is that there is evil in this world. Every human being has a free-will choice to follow God and be led by His Spirit or to follow Satan and yield to wrong spirits.

In the middle of all of this, we pray, we exercise our God-given authority to stand against the works of darkness, and we follow our Good Shepherd and hide under the shadow of His wings. We don't always get the answer to the question "why" in this life. Paul said that we "know in part" (1 Corinthians 13:9)—we don't see the whole picture—yet.

What we do know is that God is the Redeemer. That means everything that the devil has used to try to destroy your life, God can turn it around. When we run *to* God instead of *away* from God, He can take the pain, the loss, the grief, the anger, and the suffering, and He can pour out His healing power, His mercy, His grace, His love, and His strength. What were once broken and shattered pieces can now become a beautiful mosaic—a work of art that testifies of His goodness!

Don't hold God accountable for works of darkness that did not originate in Him, things that were never His will or plan for you. Let go of any anger toward Him. Release the offense and send away the heavy burden of judging and assigning blame—cast the care of it onto Him. His shoulders can carry the weight. His desire is for you to rest in Him and trust that He is for you.

> *"Come to me, all of you who are struggling and burdened, and I will give you rest. Take my yoke upon you and learn from me, because I am gentle and humble in heart, and you will find rest for your souls. For my yoke is easy, and my burden is light."*
>
> —Matthew 11:28–30 CJB

## CHAPTER 12

# Forgiving Yourself

*"And the second, like it, is this: 'You shall* ***love your neighbor as yourself****.'"*

—Mark 12:31a NKJV, emphasis mine

For some, loving God is not the issue. There is no animosity toward God, but to love and forgive yourself is the battle you face. I know this battle all too well. When we make conscious decisions to live in a way that we know is not right, and we walk away from the love of the Father, we can experience pain and loss and grief for which we usually blame ourselves. We can sometimes be our hardest judge and our own worst enemy. We sometimes tell ourselves WE should have been there, or WE could have prevented a loss, or WE failed someone in their hour of need. When we talk about living in the freedom that forgiveness brings, it's not just refusing to forgive God or forgive others that can keep us in bondage; it is also refusing to forgive ourselves.

> *If we confess our sins, He is faithful and just to forgive us our sins and to cleanse us from all unrighteousness.*
>
> —1 John 1:9 NKJV

Sometimes we fail; we fall; we make mistakes. Jesus did not come into the world to condemn the world. He came to save it. He came to cancel the debt of sin and keep God's ledger at a zero balance—His blood paid the price in full! God forgives us. God cleanses us from the stain and guilt and shame of sin. *If He can let it go, then why can't we?*

I'm not saying this is an easy task, but we must do it by faith, as we learned earlier. Our feelings may take time to catch up with our heart decision to forgive our own failures and mistakes. We may still be living in the consequences of some of those mistakes, but we must learn and grow from them. We must let go of the past so we can step into our good future. God's mercies are new every morning—every day there is fresh mercy for us! Every day!

Don't beat yourself up with the bat the devil puts in your hand. Stop hitting yourself with it and start hitting him with it! Let the truth about who you are in Christ begin to come out of your mouth. Declare that you are a new creation in Christ, that old things have passed away and all things have become new (2 Corinthians 5:17). Declare that you are God's child and the blood of Jesus has washed you clean (1 John 1:9). Tell the devil that God's plan is to prosper you, not to harm you—that your end will be good, and you will finish strong! Then tell him that his end isn't looking so good and command him to go in the name of Jesus. This will break you out of your self-imposed prison. You don't need to punish yourself. Forgive yourself and live in the freedom that Christ died for you to have.

CHAPTER 13

# Walking in Divine Love

*God has chosen you and made you his holy people. He loves you. So you should always clothe yourselves with mercy, kindness, humility, gentleness, and patience. Bear with each other and forgive each other. If someone does wrong to you,* ***forgive that person because the Lord forgave you****. Even more than all this, clothe yourself in love. Love is what holds you all together in perfect unity.*

—Colossians 3:12–14 NCV, emphasis mine

It's amazing to me how much mercy I am willing to extend to others when I am merciful to myself. It's amazing how much I can love my neighbor when I truly love myself. When I show myself patience, I am more willing to be patient with others. When I'm not holding myself to impossible standards, I won't hold others to those standards, either. When I see myself in truth—a child of God in need of His love and grace and forgiveness every day—I can look at those who are lost and without hope and have compassion on them. I can look at brothers and sisters in Christ and give them the grace to grow and mature when they say or do spiritually immature things. I can even pray for my enemies and forgive those who have hurt me.

It's God's way. Love Him with every fiber of your being and love others the way He loves you, the way He has enabled you to love yourself. Forgive the way He has forgiven you. Give freely to others the way He has given freely to you. This is a way of life. This is what it looks like to walk in divine love.

I pray that the thoughts and words in this book have helped you find a way to forgive. At the very least, I pray you would take all the truth presented here and ask God to help you start with a willing heart. I pray that wherever you find yourself on this journey, you would live in greater and greater levels of freedom as

God's truth makes you free. You can choose this very day to leave the bondage of unforgiveness behind and walk out every step by faith with the God who loves you. He is with you, and with Him all things are possible (Mark 10:27).

# About the Author

Kelli Sanders's story is not one that can be neatly packaged and tied up with tidy bows. It's messy and real and filled with God's grace. As a young single mom struggling with drug addiction, she found God as she prayed for Him to reveal Himself to her. He answered that prayer, and she was born again in the year 2000.

From 2004 through 2006, Kelli attended Bible college at The Rock School of Ministry in Southern California, and then she moved overseas to the Philippines, where she served as a missionary under Mike Keyes Ministries International.

In the summer of 2009, Kelli returned to the United States with her son, after having endured a broken and abusive marriage that ended after repeated incidents of unfaithfulness. With only a few suitcases of clothes and a word from God, they moved to Branson, Missouri, to begin the rebuilding and healing process.

It was in Branson that Kelli met her husband, Tom, and had two more beautiful children, gained a daughter-in-love, and later welcomed a precious grandbaby. For over a decade, she served the local church there, growing deep roots into the love and grace of God, gathering women and teen girls for discipleship, and planting the seeds for what is now Grow in God Ministries, a web-based ministry established with the intent to restore broken lives through a living relationship with Jesus.

Tom and Kelli now reside with their two younger children in Louisiana, where they have made The Father's House their church home.